101 ESSENT
ON MANAGING BEHAVIOU ___ EARLY YEARS

101 ESSENTIAL LIST SERIES

101 ESSENTIAL LISTS
ON MANAGING
BEHAVIOUR IN THE
EARLY YEARS

*Simon Brownhill, Fiona Shelton
and Clare Gratton*

continuum

Continuum International Publishing Group
The Tower Building   80 Maiden Lane
11 York Road   Suite 704
London   New York
SE1 7NX   NY 10038

www.continuumbooks.com   # 78886499

© Simon Brownhill, Fiona Shelton and Clare Gratton 2006

British Library Cataloguing-in-Publication Data
A catalogue record for this book is available from the British Library.

ISBN: 0–8264–8989–3 (paperback)

Library of Congress Cataloging-in-Publication Data
A catalog record for this book is available from the Library of Congress.

Typeset by YHT Ltd, London
Printed and bound in Great Britain by Ashford Colour Press,
Gosport, Hampshire

Dedications

Mum and Dad and the Fishers

SPB

Mum, Dad and John Regan

FS

Mum, Dad and Richard

CG

Acknowledgements

First and foremost we would like to thank our publishers, Continuum, and in particular Christina Garbutt for her vision in seeing the potential of this book in *Nursery Nightmares*, an article published in *Special Children* – thank you for making our publishing dreams come true!

We would also like to thank Lynn Barker, a wonderful teaching assistant whom Clare is very fortunate to work with, Karen Fisher, dedicated child minder and Simon's 'second mum', and Alison Hardman, Partnership Manager extraordinaire and fabulously witty colleague in being the critical audience for the first draft of the book – we are very grateful for all the unpaid time you devoted to 'our baby' and all your help, support and constructive advice you gave.

We would like to offer our sincere thanks to Dr Des Hewitt for kindly reviewing the final draft – your educated 'words of wisdom' have enriched and empowered our book.

We would like to thank all of the children, both past and present, whom we have come into contact with at school – without working with each and everyone of you 'little rascals' and learning how to manage your behaviour we would have never been able to write this book. Thank you for being *you*!

Finally, we would like to thank *you* for investing your hard-earned money in a copy of our book. If you can take *one* idea and use it to make a difference to your practice or to one child that you work with then it makes all of that thinking and writing we did worthwhile!

Thank you all very much.

SPB, FS and CG

Before we begin...

This book is designed to support teachers who work with children aged three to seven years. It is designed to be *general guidance* – it will not give you everything nor is it designed to do this. Clearly every behavioural issue will require different strategies depending on the child, their needs, the context in which the behaviour occurred, the time of day, etc. Most importantly the professional judgement of the teacher will clearly impact on the strategies selected and their effectiveness.

This book has been written to promote and sustain good behaviour in children, as well as addressing issues relating to poor behaviour. It is important to remember that this book will not provide you with a 'quick fix' in terms of dealing with behavioural issues in your classroom – behaviour management is *hard work* and you will need to carefully select strategies *you* feel you would be able to use with the children in *your* class and use them consistently and regularly for them to have the maximum impact.

Remember: what works for one child will not necessarily work for another. This is what makes managing children's behaviour so infinitely exciting and, at times, a little *frustrating*! So, armed with this book, go forth and make a positive difference to children's lives with the 'tools of the behaviour management trade'!

CONTENTS

CHAPTER 4: **Behaviour and the School**

CHAPTER 5: **Behaviour and Resources**

CHAPTER 6: **Behaviour, the Body and the Voice**

CHAPTER 7: **Behaviour-Management Systems**

CHAPTER 8: **Behaviour Through the Day**

Introducing Behaviour Management

 'Jack, let me introduce you to Behaviour Management. Behaviour Management, this is Jack.'

Our job as a teacher is to help children to learn. Sounds simple, doesn't it? However, there will be times when we find ourselves struggling to get children to behave appropriately.

So ... what are we meant to do?

Well ... dip into this book and you will find a wealth of practical ideas, approaches and suggestions to effectively manage the behaviour of the 'little rascals'! Here are some initial ideas to get you started:

- Always keep calm.
- Learn the children's names.
- Use humour to defuse any tension.
- Have an infectious enthusiasm for your subject, even if you hate what you are teaching!
- Always look for the good in children.
- Use praise and rewards to acknowledge good behaviour.
- Stress that it is not the *child* you dislike, it is their *behaviour*.
- Be organized.
- Be consistent.
- Behaviour is directly linked to self-esteem, so make children feel good about themselves.
- If at first you do not succeed try, try, try again: miracles do not happen overnight; you have to persevere.
- Establish clear rules and routines.

- Clearly display and refer to the school/class rules.
- Always start each day afresh – please do not hold grudges.
- Smile!

LIST 2   Every Child Matters: the philosophy of behaviour management

This book is based on a series of principles, beliefs and practices which we three authors have adopted as our philosophy of behaviour management in the classroom. Reflect on the points below and use these to build your own philosophy of behaviour management:

○ Every child should be treated fairly.
○ No child should be physically harmed by their teacher or by other children.
○ Every child should be allowed to explain themselves.
○ Every child should feel warm, secure and safe in their classroom.
○ Every child should be allowed to learn while being free from distraction.
○ Every child should be rewarded for their good behaviour.
○ Every child should know the rules of the classroom and understand the consequences if these are broken.
○ Every child should be able to recognize good behaviour in their peers and their teachers.
○ Every child should have enough self-confidence to stand up for their own rights.
○ Every child should model good behaviour in all aspects of their life, both at school and at home.
○ Every child should understand how good behaviour has a positive impact on people around them.

LIST 3   The definitive *dos* of managing behaviour

Please do ...

○ have clear, high expectations of all children which are shared with them.
○ be a good role model for behaviour.
○ identify good behaviour as and where appropriate.
○ change your rewards regularly to stimulate and motivate children.
○ give children *genuine* praise ten times more than criticism.
○ have clearly defined classroom rules and expectations and refer to them daily.
○ adhere to any agreements you make with your children.
○ use a range of individual, group and whole-class rewards.
○ give children choices.
○ be assertive when you need to be.
○ protect children's self-esteem.
○ use your voice in a calm and collected manner.
○ acknowledge children's anger and frustration.
○ ensure teaching assistants and parent helpers use the same strategies as you.
○ keep trying!
○ smile and breathe. Try to remember that the cause of the behaviour ... could be you!

LIST 4 The definitive *don'ts* of managing behaviour

Please don't ...

- ○ shout or lose your temper.
- ○ make empty threats.
- ○ take a reward away that has been given for good behaviour.
- ○ punish the whole class for one child's behaviour.
- ○ disrupt your teaching and the children's learning to control behaviour.
- ○ make a big fuss about a child's inappropriate behaviour.
- ○ make children cry on a Friday afternoon.
- ○ hold a grudge – each day should start afresh.
- ○ use derogatory nicknames for the children.
- ○ use sarcasm.
- ○ develop bad habits, e.g. 'SSSSSSSSHHHHHHHHHHHHHHH!'
- ○ leave yourself isolated with an individual child.
- ○ lower your expectations of children.
- ○ destroy the children's self-esteem.
- ○ leave the children on the 'thinking chair' for long periods of time.
- ○ grab or smack children.
- ○ cry in front of children.
- ○ chastise children in front of their peers.
- ○ refer to race, belief or physical appearance.
- ○ think it is always your fault if children are unable to behave.
- ○ give up on them!
- ○ forget you are human!

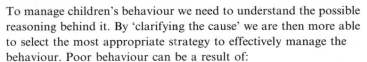

L I S T 5 Clarifying the causes

To manage children's behaviour we need to understand the possible reasoning behind it. By 'clarifying the cause' we are then more able to select the most appropriate strategy to effectively manage the behaviour. Poor behaviour can be a result of:

- poor self-esteem/self-image
- poor social/communication skills
- tiredness/exhaustion
- attitudes – personal, gender-based
- illness and conditions – medical, biological, psychological, emotional and genetic
- lack of motivation and interest
- attention seeking
- major life changes
- high adrenaline/testosterone levels
- competition/rivalry
- home influences – culture, religious, parental expectations, socio-economic
- media influences – film, radio, TV, music, computer games and Internet images
- poorly behaved role-models – children, parents, carers, guardians and teachers
- too many activities without structure – free play
- reactions to changes – temperature, smells, noise levels, amount of space available, the weather
- traumatic family incidences – bereavement, serious illness, abuse, divorce or separation
- stage of child development – age, sex, maturity, concentration levels, attention span
- poor adjustment in the classroom
- testing the boundaries – assessing how far they can challenge the teacher
- inability to cope with one's own feelings and emotions
- personality clashes with teacher and peers
- peer-group influences
- poor academic achievement.

LIST 6 Approaching behaviour management

There are many different theories relating to managing behaviour and moral development. But what are they and how can they help us to manage children's behaviour? These are just a few examples:

- ○ The style of discipline that parents adopt will have a big effect on how the children respond to you. A friendly chat with parents can help you to find out this information.
- ○ Research suggests that children respond best to an 'inductive' style of discipline which involves appealing to children's understanding rather than their emotions and fears.
- ○ Jean Piaget (1957)* believed that siblings and peers have an influence on managing behaviour – children can model behaviour to each other through collaborative projects within the school.
- ○ Research suggests that providing young children with a rationale (reasoning) for rules is more effective than punishment.
- ○ A child's conscience is developed as a result of internalizing adults' rules and values. This will be more developed in some children than others, so help children to listen to their 'inner voice' and to respond to it.
- ○ Children's moral development will be developed by telling stories that involve decision making about difficult situations and discuss the consequences of all choices.
- ○ Children are not passive in rule learning; they will actively attempt to make sense of rules by questioning, challenging and by testing the limits through deliberate non-compliance. Just grin and bear it!

* Piaget, J. (1957), *Construction of Reality in the Child*, London, Routledge & Kegan Paul.

L I S T 7   'Behave Bro!' Behaviour management phrases

Every book or article about behaviour management will be full of phrases to guide your thoughts and approaches to effective management. This book is no exception! Choose your favourites and use them to guide your own practice:

- ○ Say what you mean and mean what you say.
- ○ Remember ... no means no!
- ○ Think before you act.
- ○ Catch 'em being good.
- ○ Be firm but fair.
- ○ Never 'give as good as you get'.
- ○ Have high expectations – work to raise and maintain them.
- ○ Consistency and clarity keep kids calm.
- ○ Practise what you preach.
- ○ Always explain your actions.
- ○ Learn from others and from your own mistakes.
- ○ Be positive!
- ○ Praise others and they will praise you.
- ○ Don't do as I *say*, do as I *do*.
- ○ Avoid your heart leading your head.
- ○ Stay calm and smile.

Words and terms

Everything you read about behaviour management is full of words
and terms which you are expected to know and understand. Below
are just some of the terminologies you may come across linked to
behaviour management – how many of these do you know, use and
understand?

- ○ behaviour modification
- ○ discipline
- ○ positivity
- ○ purposeful praise
- ○ motivation
- ○ self-esteem
- ○ recognizing success
- ○ establishing rules
- ○ non-verbal gestures
- ○ instilling manners
- ○ self-discipline
- ○ environment
- ○ monitoring
- ○ establishing expectations
- ○ confrontations
- ○ achievement
- ○ attainment
- ○ boundaries
- ○ effort levels
- ○ points of view
- ○ establishing the ethos
- ○ climate
- ○ role models
- ○ equal opportunities
- ○ formulating routines
- ○ incentives
- ○ issuing sanctions
- ○ offering support
- ○ rewards
- ○ responsibilities
- ○ fairness
- ○ preventative measures

- respect
- acceptable attitudes
- protocols
- contract
- punishments
- misbehaviour
- constructive criticism
- intervention
- conflict
- orders and instructions
- reprimands
- privileges

Identify terms you are unclear about and work to develop your understanding of them.

Children's questions

We sometimes get so involved in managing children's behaviour and lesson planning, and assessing and actually teaching that we forget how wonderful children are. Each child is unique and so are some of the questions they ask us:

- If beauty is skin deep, then how deep is ugly?
- How do pigs lay bacon?
- Why is a duck's nose his mouth?
- Do sausages grow, or are they born?
- Miss, does it hurt to be old?
- Why do they collect money on a plate in church? Does the vicar eat it?
- Why am I always sticky?
- When you get married do you have to divorce your mummy first?
- Why do you have hairy legs? Did your daddy get you from the zoo?
- Why does time go fast when you are having fun?
- Why is there always a spoon at the bottom of the bowl after you have done the washing up?
- Are squirrels just faster hamsters which have escaped?
- Aren't you married because you love yourself too much, miss?

Behaviour and the Child | 2

LIST 10   Child development

Child development is a vast area of research and requires extensive study to secure understanding. It is, however, worth remembering that all children are different and progress at different rates, which makes it difficult to predict exactly what to expect from children at particular ages. But how do children develop an understanding of what constitutes good behaviour?

Fisher (1995)* suggests that children have three rationales for different kinds of rules: *moral* – 'You should not kill', *conventional* – 'You should wear clothes to school', and *practical* – 'You should brush your teeth every day'. Try to use these rationales to explore what rules are important in the school environment.

Although Piaget (1957) believed that children up to the age of four have no understanding of rules, other researchers believe that if children are given an explanation for consequences of poor behaviour, their behaviour improves. Therefore, rules must be explicit and you must be consistent in applying them.

Talking about fairness and justice with young children helps them, in most cases, to regulate their thinking, and consequently their behaviour. Alongside this, social experience plays an integral part in moral development. Teachers are therefore encouraged to provide these kinds of opportunities for children on a regular basis to ensure theoretical prospectives on behaviour management have a practical and positive effect in the classroom.

* Fisher, R. (1995), *Teaching Children to Learn*, Cheltenham, Nelson Thornes.

LIST 11 The 'Good': appropriate forms of behaviour

We use the term 'good' a great deal in school. For children to demonstrate 'good' behaviour we need to be clear about the behaviours we wish to promote in our classrooms. Ensure that children know which behaviours are being commented on when they are being 'good' – the list below offers desirable behaviours in children:

- interested
- motivated
- kind and considerate
- honest
- team-player
- polite
- confident
- helpful
- turn-taker
- curious
- good listener
- able to share
- suitably independent
- risk taker
- concentrates well
- self-aware
- well-mannered
- empathetic
- open
- warm
- happy
- proud and, most importantly,
- a decent human being.

Consider how you promote these behaviours in your classroom.

LIST 12

The 'Bad and the Ugly': inappropriate behaviours in the classroom

While there are behaviours we must encourage in our classrooms, there are also behaviours that we need to ensure children understand as inappropriate. The list below identifies some common undesirable behaviours:

- aggressive tendencies
- attention-seeking
- bullying tendencies
- anxiousness
- mood swings
- being tearful
- defiance
- lying
- name-calling
- swearing
- spitting
- shouting and calling out
- lashing out with hands and feet
- biting
- pinching
- being disrespectful
- day-dreaming
- arrogance
- making silly noises
- being impolite
- poor manners
- fighting
- stealing
- deliberately damaging/ruining peer's work.

A number of the behaviours above can be a child's response to poor teaching. Consider how you discourage children from using these behaviours in your classroom.

LIST 13   Influencing behaviour

Every day, children have to deal with a wide range of problems, situations and external influences before they arrive at school. All of these can affect their behaviour and we need to be aware of them.

- A lack of breakfast/nutrition – hungry children always find it difficult to concentrate/behave.
- Poor diet – junk/processed food has a negative influence on concentration and behaviour.
- Arguments between parents/carers.
- Sibling rivalry.
- Having older siblings with behavioural problems.
- New baby – this can cause feelings of insecurity/jealousy.
- Busy mornings – parents/carers sleeping in.
- Lack of sleep – late nights and early mornings are never a good combination.
- TVs and DVDs – violent programmes can encourage violent/ abusive behaviour.
- Medication – some prescription medications affect behaviour.
- Poor parenting skills – behaviour at home may not be managed effectively or appropriately.
- Lack of positive role models – if everyone at home behaves inappropriately then where is appropriate behaviour learnt? That one is over to you!

LIST 14 — *How do you feel inside?* Behaviour and self-esteem

Children need to feel good about themselves in order to be happy, to be able to socialize effectively and to achieve. Building self-esteem should be an essential part of education. Children with high self-esteem are more likely to:

○ smile
○ be happy
○ be secure in who they are
○ socialize with a wide variety of people in a range of situations
○ behave appropriately
○ cope well with change and be flexible enough to deal with any situation
○ take on board new ideas
○ be reliable
○ be responsible
○ guide and support other children in the acquisition of new skills
○ be confident enough to speak in front of the class/group/other individuals
○ have belief in themselves and believe they are capable of achieving their goals
○ act as a role-model for others
○ take on a challenge
○ strive for success.

Refer to Chapter 9, *Behaviour-Management Strategies*, for ideas and suggestions as to how to raise children's self-esteem in the classroom.

LIST 15 *How do children learn?* Learning styles in the classroom

Children can become frustrated, restless and bored when they feel they are not doing or achieving which can lead to behaviour problems. We all have preferred ways of learning. How well do you know the learners in your class?

○ Plan for multi-sensory lessons to benefit all children.

○ Give all children, particularly those of a low ability, the opportunity to work in their own way. They will understand their own thought process better than yours.

○ Model 'think alouds' to the children so they can hear how you work out problems. Link this with gestures, written words and simple flow-charts.

○ Give children opportunities to make some decisions about the choices they make in their work. They will become independent and self-sufficient.

○ If children believe they can do something well they will enjoy their work more. Remember: self-efficacy is the key to learning.

○ Allow children to work in their learning style, e.g. kinaesthetic, but do not limit them to this; it is important to help them to develop other ways of working.

○ Really get to know your children and draw on their interests in your planning.

○ During carpet activities plan a variety of looking, listening and doing to keep the children involved as much as possible.

○ Make sure signs and notices have words and pictures.

LIST 16   Checklist for the child

When things go wrong and one of your 'little rascals' is behaving inappropriately, encourage them to manage their own behaviour by teaching them to ask themselves the following:

- Am I angry?
- Am I shouting?
- Are my words hurtful or horrible?
- Do I feel hot?
- Is my heart beating quickly?
- Am I hurting other people?
- Do I need to move away from others?
- Do I need to stop?
- Do I need to sit quietly?
- Do I need to run on the spot to stop feeling cross?
- Am I breathing slowly?
- Do I need to close my eyes?
- Can I count to ten and then think?
- Am I calm and quiet?
- Am I ready to talk to others?
- Have I made someone sad?
- Do I know what I have done wrong?
- Do I need to say sorry?

LIST 17   Expecting the unexpected

Like children's behaviour in the classroom, you never quite know *what* will happen next ...

- Inappropriate items brought in for 'show and tell' – daddy's wallet stuffed full of money and women's phone numbers, mummy's pink fluffy handcuffs, Gran's kidney stone, final reminder from the gas board, Cutie the *dead* hamster.
- Unusual requests from parents – 'Can she have a new book, because her *dad* drew all over it?', a numerical score on the end-of-year report to indicate where the child is ranked in the class, a written explanation of how/why a child got nits.
- Things you have no control over – the weather on Sports Day, the fire alarm during SATs week, nits, the coach company turning up on time, children's bladders five minutes after the last toilet stop.
- Children's comments about their teachers – 'I like your hair, sir! It looks like my Granddad's!', 'Why are you wearing perfume, miss? Do you smell?'

Behaviour and the Teacher

LIST 18   'Prepared, patient and positive!' Personal teacher qualities

To manage behaviour we need to have a range of ideal personal qualities which will allow us to be effective. Take a look at this list and consider which qualities apply to you, and which you need to develop. Are you:

- ○ kind?
- ○ caring?
- ○ considerate?
- ○ patient?
- ○ firm but fair?
- ○ a good listener?
- ○ respectful?
- ○ understanding?
- ○ flexible?
- ○ attentive?
- ○ supportive?
- ○ thoughtful?
- ○ knowledgeable?
- ○ consistent?
- ○ a learner?
- ○ approachable?
- ○ warm?
- ○ organized?
- ○ accommodating?
- ○ interested?
- ○ confident?
- ○ in control?
- ○ a leader?
- ○ a team-player?
- ○ energetic?
- ○ committed?

- vibrant?
- courteous?
- a turn-taker?
- able to share?
- sensitive?
- well planned?
- independent?
- imaginative?
- willing to take risks?
- a role model?
- intelligent?
- positive?
- trustworthy?
- secure in your own abilities?
- capable?
- encouraging?
- alert?
- calm?
- articulate?

Remember: you cannot possibly be all of the above all of the time – you are human after all!

What do you *really* think about behaviour? Teacher's attitudes towards behaviour management

Your attitude towards behaviour management has a direct impact on the way you deal with incidences in the classroom. Regarding behavioural issues as 'another thing to have to deal with' usually results in teachers managing behaviour ineffectively. A positive attitude will make all the difference!

❑ You have already started being positive – you have bought this book to help you! Buy others to support your practice.

❑ Never suffer in silence! Talk to other teachers, not only in your school but in other schools – you are not alone!

❑ Adopt an optimistic approach to behaviour management – *think* positive and positive things *will* happen.

❑ Believe in what you are doing – ask your headteacher or a colleague to watch you teaching, and allow them to offer suggestions on alternative strategies and ways to improve your behaviour management.

❑ Attend courses, conferences, seminars and training about behaviour management – you will always learn something new!

❑ If you see or hear of a strategy which you feel will not work in your class, avoid being critical about it – adapt features of it so that it *will* work.

❑ Reward *yourself* when the behaviour in your class has been good. Think about what *you* did to make your children be so good.

LIST 20 Team spirit

Days are busy, and there are often too many jobs to get through. If adults in your school pull together as a team then the mountains don't seem quite so high to climb.

- Make everyone feel involved by discussing behaviour issues with them.
- Encourage everyone to be flexible, and be happy to do someone else's tasks or share their tasks with others.
- Make sure you meet regularly to discuss whole-team issues.
- Involve parents/carers as much as possible. Giving them a sense of purpose will encourage them to return.
- When adult helpers/students arrive in school, always have an initial discussion and make clear the ethos of the school, the behaviour policy and issues of confidentiality.
- Have a welcome booklet for all new team members. Let this include all the 'basics', e.g. rules, routines, daily tasks, etc.
- Lead by example. If you are part of the team then be happy to 'roll up your sleeves' when needed.
- Ensure everyone is thanked for their efforts, no matter how small.
- Build team spirit though smiles, talk and laughter.

L I S T 21   Building relationships

Schools are very busy places and we work and deal with lots of different people every day. It is very important that we learn to get on with these people so that our relationships are successful and our lives less stressful. To build effective relationships remember to:

- smile a lot!
- make eye contact
- be interested in other people
- value everyone's opinions
- attempt to see all points of view, even those which differ from your own
- listen to others
- ask questions
- contribute to group discussion and declare your interest
- actively encourage working as a team and create situations to enable this to happen, e.g. regular meetings with all staff members present, sharing workload, etc.
- suggest your own ideas
- remember people's birthdays and celebrate them, both staff and children!
- play with children and involve yourself in their world
- encourage children to bring in items from home to share with you and the class. Let them know that you are interested in their lives
- use praise all day every day, even in the face of adversity!

LIST 22 *What sort of teacher are you? Teaching styles*

How we teach has a direct influence on how we view and react to behavioural difficulties in our classrooms. Ask yourself these questions:

○ Are you assertive enough? Don't be a 'pushover' – state your expectations and be prepared to back up your words with actions.

○ Do you feel inadequate or intimidated when a child misbehaves? Don't take it personally; look at it as a 'new challenge'.

○ Do you let your heart rule your head? If you are having a bad day, do not let it show – maintain your professionalism at all times.

○ Are you the 'Talking Leader' or 'Follower'? You have two ears and one mouth – try to use them in that ratio.

○ Formal or informal teaching styles? Strike a balance between the two, using the styles in response to children's behaviour.

○ Whole-class or individual? Plan for a balance of whole-class, group, paired and individual work in class.

○ Play or work? Play *is* work and children *do* learn through it – integrate play into your main teaching and the children's learning activities.

LIST 23 Me? A 'role model'?

Sometimes we need to show children how to behave. We can do this by showing good behaviour in the way *we* conduct *ourselves* in the classroom. The ability to model this as an example for children to replicate is an important and invaluable tool in demonstrating and therefore encouraging appropriate behaviour.

❍ Modelling can be used with the whole class or with individuals.

❍ Sometimes it is appropriate to tell the children to 'listen and do'.

❍ Sometimes it is more effective simply to behave appropriately without passing comment.

❍ If children are surrounded by positive modelling all the time their behaviour will hopefully begin to model yours and as a result will become a learned behaviour.

❍ If you expect children not to shout, then avoid shouting at them. It is always much more effective to remain calm, quiet and focused when speaking to a child about their behaviour.

❍ Model walking around school. If you are quiet, calm and sensible the children should behave similarly.

❍ Model sitting on the carpet. Always begin to talk to the children when you are sitting still, looking directly at them with your arms folded. Unfold them when you have their attention: children will recognize this as good listening behaviour.

❍ Train children to model positive behaviour for others, e.g. 'Let's show Matthew how to sit beautifully.'

❍ Use phrases like 'Don't *tell* me, *show* me'.

LIST 24   **Reactions and responses**

Every teacher will experience a range of behaviours in their classroom every day. Each child and the behaviour they exhibit will be different and we need to develop strategies and appropriate reactions and responses to deal with behavioural difficulties which come our way.

- ○ Ignore negative behaviour and praise the positive. It is not always possible to ignore behaviour, but *sometimes* it is more appropriate not to comment on it.
- ○ Praise positive behaviour with a smile/wink/thumbs up.
- ○ Tell the child you will speak to them when *they* have calmed down.
- ○ Ask the child to explain what they did and why – *is it because they cannot do the work?* Discuss the behaviour, not the child.
- ○ Sometimes it is appropriate for you to walk away and calm down before returning to deal with the behavioural issue.
- ○ Tell the child that you will speak to them once *you* have calmed down. This will give the child thinking time and allow you to deal with the rest of the class/group first.
- ○ Overreact and you run the risk of making a difficult situation worse – do allow *yourself* thinking time before you act!

L I S T 2 5   Stresses and strains: managing personal emotions

We all know children have 'off' days, but then again so do we.

- ○ Be aware of the pressure points in the school year and plan ahead for them.
- ○ At playtime, go outside and have some fresh air.
- ○ Spend five minutes planning some treats for yourself; even if they don't happen you will smile while you think of them.
- ○ If you are feeling anxious in the classroom, stop everybody and sit together on the carpet for some silent reflection if appropriate.
- ○ On difficult days, go into role; forget who you are and your problems for that short time as you take on the role of 'Pirate Pete' or 'Burglar Bill'.
- ○ If you cannot confide in a colleague about what is troubling you, write it down – it helps to get it off your chest.
- ○ Ask the children to tell you some jokes (choose your 'jokers' carefully!).
- ○ Change your plans for the day ahead – if you cannot cope with what you planned you can always do it tomorrow.
- ○ Avoid 'taking it out' on the children – it is not necessarily their fault. Although . . . !

LIST 26 · *Is there anyone out there to help me?* Using outside agencies

It is important to remember that we are never alone in terms of trying to manage children's behaviour – there are many different people, organizations, procedures and support materials out there to help us help our children:

- other teaching staff in school
- headteacher
- Special Educational Needs Coordinator
- teaching assistants
- midday supervisors
- parents and carers
- educational psychologists and psychiatrists
- speech therapists
- Local Authority
- school nurse
- health visitors
- behavioural support teams
- behavioural units
- hospitals
- doctors
- police
- national schemes, e.g. Beat Bullying
- academic literature, e.g. *Getting the buggers to behave* (3rd edition) by Sue Cowley, *100 Ideas for Managing Behaviour* by Johnnie Young (both published by Continuum).
- practical teaching guides, e.g. this one!
- journals, e.g. *BERA, Journal of Early Childhood*
- magazine publications, e.g. *Special Children*
- websites, e.g. www.behaviour4learning.co.uk.

L I S T 2 7   **Checklist for the teacher**

When all goes wrong, as it inevitably will, and one of your 'little rascals' begins to behave inappropriately, we need to check that *we* are dealing with their behaviour appropriately. Before you react it is important to stop, take a deep breath and ask yourself:

- ❑ What do I already know about the child and the situation before I react?
- ❑ Am I calm?
- ❑ Am I in control?
- ❑ Do I need to take a couple more deep breaths before I deal with this?
- ❑ Do I know all the facts? Is the situation clear to me, or do I need to ask questions?
- ❑ Is the child calm and ready to be spoken to, or do I need to control and calm the situation first?

While managing the behaviour, consider the following:

- ❑ Am I at eye-level with the child and can look directly at them?
- ❑ Is the child looking at me?
- ❑ Is my voice calm?
- ❑ Is my voice quiet?
- ❑ Is my voice steady?
- ❑ Is my voice firm?
- ❑ Am I being fair?

Afterwards, ask yourself:

- ❑ Did I sanction appropriately?
- ❑ Was I clear enough?
- ❑ Does the child understand what I said?
- ❑ Does the child now know exactly what behaviour is expected of them?
- ❑ Does the child know that they now have the opportunity to start afresh?

'Going back to the beginning': teaching children 'the facts'

Although children need to develop skills and attitudes, their own subject knowledge and understanding is also very important. Children's misconceptions can, at times, be quite hilarious.

○ Red, orange, yellow, green, black, indigo and violet are all colours of the rectum.

○ To have a baby all a cow has to do is moo and it just sort of plops out.

○ CO_2 is carbon and oxygin. H_2O is lots of gin with a bit of water in it.

○ The sun and the moon were once married but they split up so they only come out when the other one goes to bed.

○ A camel is made out of half a caramel bar.

○ Plants choke if they smell perfume.

○ The ring around the planet Saturn is its big belly.

○ Making up the truth means it's all right.

○ A triangle is a square that's gone wrong.

○ Henry the Eighth had six knives and lots of other cutlery.

○ The earth spins around on its axle.

○ Caterpillars turn into Christians.

○ Blood is pumped around the body by the lungs. The heart is just there to make you feel 'fruity'.

○ Apparently Jesus was castrated on the cross.

Behaviour and the School 4

LIST 29 — Making behaviour work in the workplace

Well-behaved children make teaching easy! Poorly behaved children make teaching an unpleasant experience. For behaviour to work to your advantage in school, you need to ensure that the following are in place:

- Get the ethos right! The school ethos will have a direct impact as to whether the behaviour in school will be good or challenging. Ensure the school ethos is warm, positive and rewarding.
- Adopt the 'team approach' to managing behaviour! Everyone who works in the school should have a common understanding about how they want children to behave in the school.
- Consistency is everything! Ensure that the ways in which good behaviour is promoted and poor behaviour is managed are consistent throughout the whole school.
- Establish that behaviour policy! Write an effective behaviour policy, and effective behaviour will come your way.
- Never stand still! Encourage everyone to find/devise new systems and strategies to promote good behaviour in the classroom.
- Believe there is good in children and they will believe there is good in you!
- See the big picture! Ensure the mission statement of the school promotes good behaviour so that it is part of all that you and the children do. Remind yourself and the children of it regularly.

LIST 30   Policy into practice

Every school should have a behaviour policy which clearly establishes the boundaries of what is acceptable, a hierarchy of sanctions for consistent and fair application and explicit rewards for good behaviour. Consider the following to ensure policy-making and practice are effective:

- ○ Ensure the policy includes the aims of the school, its mission statement, code of conduct and its values and beliefs.
- ○ Everyone who will turn the policy into practice in school needs to contribute to its production. This includes governors, the headteacher, teachers, teaching assistants and midday supervisors for example.
- ○ Ensure the rules in the policy are short, specific and realistic.
- ○ Ensure the policy is designed to help children to achieve their full potential – clarify ways in which the school will promote this.
- ○ Supply teachers, visitors and after-school clubs should be given a copy of the policy, or at least a summary of the policy for consistency purposes.
- ○ Policies should be made available for parents to access at any time.
- ○ Consider effective ways for parents to be made aware of the contents of the policy, e.g. produce a parent-friendly version of the policy, create a home–school agreement about behaviour in school, conduct a parents/guardians evening about the policy.
- ○ Ensure *you* are aware of the contents of the policy before you teach – inconsistent approaches breed bad behaviour!
- ○ Ensure the policy has a review date.

Rules and routines

To successfully manage behaviour and create a calm classroom, rules and routines are essential. Everybody in the classroom needs to know what these rules and routines are, and when they should be applied.

- ○ Ensure that everybody is involved when formulating the rules; you need a coherent approach in which everybody has a voice.
- ○ Keep the rules simple and write them in a child-friendly manner.
- ○ Limit the number of rules for maximum effectiveness.
- ○ Explain what is meant by the rule, or ask the children to explain it to you, so you are sure everybody understands.
- ○ Reinforce the rules regularly and consolidate them by applying them to yourself.
- ○ Display the rules at an appropriate height and size for the children.
- ○ Use pictures and signs alongside words and phrases.
- ○ Practise routines regularly at the start of the term.
- ○ Make learning about rules and routines fun; accompany them with songs, sound and music.
- ○ When routines become ineffective return to the basics and remind everybody of the stages.
- ○ Keep rules short and snappy so they are easy to remember.

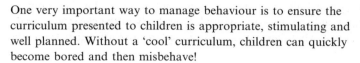

LIST 32 The 'cool' curriculum

One very important way to manage behaviour is to ensure the curriculum presented to children is appropriate, stimulating and well planned. Without a 'cool' curriculum, children can quickly become bored and then misbehave!

- Share and review learning objectives for each lesson.
- Differentiate work to meet individual needs.
- Plan for extension activities where appropriate.
- Avoid 'floating' time.
- Teach some of the foundation subjects (art and design, history, ICT) in the morning, particularly PE.
- Plan for Literacy and Numeracy to be delivered in the afternoon.
- Undertake a thematic approach to your planning.
- Plan for lots of speaking and listening activities.
- Link learning to children's interests and hobbies.
- Deliver lessons in small 'chunks'.
- Teach in a multi-sensory style.
- Integrate play into your main and independent activities.
- Use cross-curricular links to strengthen learning and teaching.
- Plan for themed days/weeks.
- Be creative – use role-play, film, PE, art and design, drama, dance.
- Allow children to teach their peers, e.g. skills, knowledge.
- Teach through story and song.
- Avoid always writing on plain A4 paper – use shaped, coloured and textured papers and card.
- Team-teach with teaching assistants, parent helpers, student trainees and outside agencies, using them to enrich delivery and content of your curriculum.

Tinkering with the timetable

Organizing the timetable is very important to ensure there is breadth and balance to children's learning. Flexibility with timetables will allow you to respond positively to children's behaviour.

- Whenever the hall is free, use it!
- Try to deliver activities in different parts of the school, e.g. on the field, on the playground, in the corridor, in the staffroom.
- Teach art and design to calm the children when appropriate. Use drama and dance to liven up lethargic bodies!
- Team-teach with other teachers.
- Plan for subjects to be taught simultaneously so the children are kept motivated.
- Deliver subject knowledge by linking it to children's interests.
- Swap classes with other teachers for the morning.
- Deliver part of a lesson and then return to it later on in the day.
- Plan for midday supervisors to work with the children in class where and when appropriate.
- Play to the strengths of your staff. Observe a colleague teaching their curriculum strength, and return the favour.
- Organize timetables to allow different year groups to work together – Year 2 working alongside Foundation 1 children in the library.

L I S T 3 4 Experimenting with the environment

The classroom environment can play a major part in promoting good behaviour in children. If it appears to be unplanned, disorganized and messy then you run the risk of children misbehaving.

○ Ensure that the environment is clean and welcoming to children and parents/carers.
○ Try to keep surfaces clutter free.
○ Experiment with different layouts for the tables and chairs.
○ Rearrange the layout of the classroom every half-term/term.
○ Allow displays to go outside of the border.
○ Create tabletop displays with objects for children to touch, smell and explore.
○ Ensure your desk does not take up valuable learning and teaching space. Do you really need a desk?
○ Ensure children can move easily around the room.
○ Ensure the room is adequately lit with natural light and the temperature is suitable.
○ Ensure the room is well ventilated and there is plenty of fresh air.
○ Plan for small areas for private individual work and social interaction.
○ Use the space provided by windows, window sills and the ceiling.
○ Plan for activities for certain areas of the room, e.g. floor space, tabletop space, around a display, in the wet area, near to an electrical point.
○ Ask children to help organize the environment.

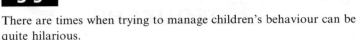

LIST 35 Should I laugh or cry?

There are times when trying to manage children's behaviour can be quite hilarious.

Teacher: Has anyone heard something said about someone which was not very nice?
Child: Yeah! That you're a big fat pig!

Teacher: Why it is important to behave?
Child: Because you'll have a paddy if we don't!

Teacher: Clare, your behaviour has been *excellent*!
Child: Thanks, Miss. I could not be bothered to misbehave today!

Teacher: Why do you think it is not nice to pick your nose, Jack?
Child: Because your head will cave in, Miss!

Child: Sir, Craig has just kicked me in the *balls*!
Teacher: James, please do not use language like that!
Child: Sorry. Craig kicked me in the 'toilet area' and it *bloody* hurt!

Teacher: Kim, I like you but you're –
Child: 'A pain in the arse', miss?
Teacher: Well, I would not put it *quite* like that ...

A Year 1 child is sent to a teacher with a note. 'What's this?' asks the teacher. The child replies 'It says "I'm being a little bugger and Mrs Kindle is going to kill me if you don't take me off her hands!" I read it to save you time reading it!'

Behaviour and Resources

LIST 36 Range of resources

We know that resources are useful and important, but what kind of resources do we need/how many do we need and why? All of these questions need to be answered when considering how the use and type of resources might affect children's behaviour.

- ○ Always ensure there are enough! If children have constant access to what they need, disruption will be minimized and children are more likely to just 'get on'.
- ○ Consider whether the resources provided fit the need/purpose.
- ○ Use natural as well as manufactured resources.
- ○ Provide choice to promote independence and individuality.
- ○ Limit choice. Sometimes providing a wide range of pens/writing equipment is too much for children.
- ○ Make it clear which resources are available for the children to select independently and which are not.
- ○ Encourage self-selection by keeping all of the scissors/pencils/ rulers for example together in the same place. Make sure everyone knows where they 'live'.
- ○ Teach which resources best fit the need, and let children explore the options.
- ○ Ask children which resources they need to 'do the job'.

Respecting and valuing resources

Resources make our teaching and the children's learning more accessible and enjoyable. However, as they can be quite expensive, children need to be taught how to respect and value resources to build a sense of ownership and responsibility in the classroom.

- ○ Use colourful and quality resources which children will want to use.
- ○ Praise children's appropriate use of resources.
- ○ Make your resources 'real', by giving them a 'home' where they 'live'.
- ○ Keep resources accessible only to adults, in high and hidden places.
- ○ Make groups and individuals responsible for caring for resources.
- ○ Allow staff and children to decide on the resources they would like to use.
- ○ Buy resources together.
- ○ Share and borrow resources from other classes, other schools and from home.
- ○ Use adult education centres and traveller support services for additional resources.
- ○ Send resources home as and where appropriate.

The rules of resources

In order to manage behaviour we need to make the use of resources easy, constructive and stress-free for children! We need clear rules! Here are some ideas of how to do it:

○ set the rules together
○ make sure everyone knows the rules and why we need them
○ put the rules on the wall and refer to them regularly.

Let the rules include:

○ always return resources
○ return resources to the correct place
○ return resources in the condition you would wish to find them
○ use resources carefully
○ remind any children who are not using resources carefully to do so
○ make sure the resources you are using are the right ones for the job
○ take care when moving around the classroom with resources
○ take care when using resources. Some resources can be dangerous if used incorrectly.

Use these ideas to formulate your own rules for resources and their appropriate use.

Organizing resources

Organization is the key to the successful running of any classroom. If you effectively organize your resources, your children will be easier to manage and your days will be calmer and the children's behaviour more appropriate.

- Encourage children to label their own resources. If they have written the labels themselves, they are much more likely to respect the system.
- Label resources on all sides.
- Place photographs or drawings the children have taken/made on resource boxes and on the walls/shelves, so that it is clear to them where each resource is kept.
- Make it clear how many of each resource there are by labelling boxes and pots with the relevant number.
- Make someone responsible for checking if the resources are in the correct place and that there is the correct amount of each resource. Make time during the day to collect/return/check/tidy resources.
- Store resources in stackable, easily accessible containers.
- Keep all your resources in one place and always in the same place.
- Never mix two different sets of resources as this will cause unnecessary confusion.

LIST 40   Storing resources

If resources are effectively organized then it is just as important that they are stored effectively. An organized classroom always helps when managing behaviour.

○ Use a range of pots, tins, tubs, boxes and trays.
○ Preferably use storage equipment that stacks as this takes up less tabletop space.
○ Resources to be used by the children need to be easily accessible. Place these in containers without lids.
○ Have a resource cupboard for the surplus resources and use these to replace ones that children use every day.
○ Resources accessed only occasionally can be placed in large, stackable boxes to save space.
○ Ask your caretaker to build shelves high on a wall for equipment which is used half-termly, and low down for resources which children access independently on a daily basis.
○ Respect your storage equipment. Clean boxes, etc. every year to keep your resources in tip-top condition.
○ Have a wash day where everyone joins in the fun. These sorts of days are best undertaken in the summer, at the end of term, outside in the sunshine with buckets, brushes and soapy water!

LIST 41 Accessing resources

Thinking about where to put resources is another important aspect of managing your classroom and therefore children's behaviour. Ask yourself: *Where* shall I put it? *Who* is going to use it? *When* will they use it?

○ Use window sills. These are very easily accessible and often forgotten about; most pots and boxes perfectly fit on sills.

○ Build or buy shelves that can be positioned to come 'out of' the wall. This will segment your classroom and allow access to resources from both sides of the shelves.

○ Consider whether it makes more sense to store resources on tables/at workstations or in a central location for all the children to access when necessary.

○ Think about storing some resources outside. Large building equipment could be kept in a shed, which would free up space inside. More space means children can move around easier and are less likely to be in each other's space.

○ Share resources! To encourage this, store play equipment, etc. in a central location that can be accessed by more than one class.

LIST 42 — Setting out resources

If we have the resources and we know how and when we want them to be used, the next thing we need to consider is how we want to present them to the children. Consider the following approaches to managing behaviour when setting resources out:

○ Ensure you set the resources out and make them appealing to the children.
○ Let the children set them out, under your guidance.
○ Consider carefully which resources to put on which table.
○ Give the children completely free choice. If they can access it, they can use it. This will promote independence and child-centred learning.
○ Provide some 'free choice' areas and others with pre-selected equipment in them.
○ Use photographs to show the children which resources are available to them during a session/day and allow them to access these independently.
○ Always give clear instructions.
○ Expect ALL the children to listen to the 'setting out' instructions and expect them ALL to take responsibility for the task.
○ Ensure resources are set out appropriately before beginning a task/play activity.
○ Encourage the children to recognize how the resources are set out before beginning the activity, so that they can tidy them away appropriately when the activity is finished.

L I S T 4 3 Tidying away resources

Once we are properly organized and our resources have been set out and used appropriately it is time to tidy away, and this part is just as important. Consider the following approaches to managing behaviour when tidying:

○ Model effective tidying.
○ Tidy away some resources independently of the children.
○ Tell the children you like 'tidiers' who check labels, count resources, take care, etc.
○ Let the children tidy away under your guidance.
○ When giving instructions about tidying away, give named jobs to individuals and encourage all the children to listen so that they are all responsible for the job being done.
○ Clearly state a 'tidying job' and then clearly state whom you want to do that job.
○ Tell the children WHAT you expect them to do, HOW you expect them to do it and WHERE you want the resources to go.
○ Once instructions have been given, stand back and watch. The children will get used to you doing this and will know that you expect the job to be done.
○ Encourage children to observe each other tidying, and encourage them to share the positive aspects of their observations.
○ Praise terrific tidying!

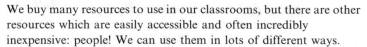

LIST 44 Using human resources

We buy many resources to use in our classrooms, but there are other resources which are easily accessible and often incredibly inexpensive: people! We can use them in lots of different ways.

- ○ Parents. Use them to practise reading. If parents value their children's education then children are much more likely to have a positive view of school.
- ○ Younger and older siblings. Encourage children to read to younger and older brothers and sisters, and be read to by them. Learning should be made fun and a part of family life and this will raise the child's self-esteem.
- ○ Harness interests. Is there a Granddad who knows all about steam trains? Ask him to talk to the children. They will love it – what a brilliant reward for positive behaviour!
- ○ Sticker charts. Continue these with the adults at home to make parents and children aware of positive behaviour management.
- ○ Had a whole day/week of brilliant behaviour? Ask the headteacher to visit the children and share a favourite story as a treat.
- ○ Trainees. There are a range of student trainees who come as part of their course or on a voluntary basis. Ensure they are actively involved in the learning and teaching which takes place as opposed to sharpening the pencils all the time!
- ○ Children. The children are resources in themselves! Point out children who are behaving beautifully, caring for resources, being kind and generous. Use these children to exemplify expectations!

Behaviour, the Body and the Voice

 'I don't want to be here!' Reading and responding to body language

We can read a lot about the mood of children by the way they hold themselves. Reading body language can be very useful in preventing unwanted and inappropriate behaviour in the classroom.

○ Folded arms can be a sign of defence or defiance; encourage children to open up by showing you are interested in them.

○ Clasped hands can be a sign of anxiety or frustration; point out things the child is doing or has done well to help them to relax.

○ Sitting bolt upright and occupying a small space is a sign of feeling guarded; encourage children to talk about their interests and themselves.

○ Looking up and to the right or left indicates remembering something or being deep in imaginative thought; watch your children carefully, you might not want to disturb them!

○ Children who use their hands when they talk are confident and enthusiastic. What do *you* do when *you* talk?

○ Not maintaining eye contact can be a sign of boredom, but it could also be a sign of shyness; try to show interest in a child to help them to overcome this.

○ Pointing can be perceived as aggressive behaviour; be aware of what you model to the children.

LIST 46 Physical contact: the facts

Avoid unnecessary physical contact with children wherever possible. Innocent actions can be misconstrued. All schools should have a policy on physical restraint and training is available. Refer to school policy and to LEA guidelines if you are unsure.

❍ Children have the right not to be touched, and this is important to remember.
❍ It is the duty of the school to maintain the child's welfare.
❍ A member of staff should be trained in this area.
❍ Physical restraint should *always* be the last resort.

If you have to use physical restraint, remember:

❍ It must be deemed to be reasonable by the teacher.
❍ Reasonable restraint might mean: in self-defence, where danger is imminent or where injury may be caused to another or themselves.
❍ Do not restrain a child in a way that might cause injury.
❍ Ensure the child knows that you are restraining them for their own welfare.
❍ Report all incidents of physical restraint through school procedure including type of restraint, reason for restraint, date and time of incident.
❍ *Never* use other children in the restraint.
❍ Where possible, risk-assess the situation, the environment, the medical considerations, etc.

Please do check current national recommendations relating to this area of behaviour management.

L I S T 4 7 Flexible faces

Our face can be a powerful resource in managing children's behaviour – a single expression can say a thousand words, one of them being 'behave'! Use a mirror to experiment with these different features of your face:

- ○ *Eyebrows* – raise them to express surprise, lower them when you are displeased.
- ○ *Mouth* – close your mouth when you want children to stop talking, open it when you wish to express shock, horror or surprise.
- ○ *Smile* – practise different smiles to show how happy you are with the children.
- ○ *Lips* – thin the lips when you are disappointed, plump them when you are happy.
- ○ *Cheeks* – raise the cheeks when you are pleased.
- ○ *Nose* – look down the nose to convey disappointment.
- ○ *Straight face* – avoid making any expression to show disappointment.

Combine these facial expressions to convey the following messages:

- ○ Stop that at once!
- ○ Well done! I am very proud of you!
- ○ I am surprised you just did that!
- ○ I think you can try harder than that!
- ○ Come on! Try it one more time!
- ○ I will not wait any longer for you!
- ○ Sit up, please!
- ○ Thank you very much!

L I S T 4 8   Various voices

The voice is the most precious resource for all teachers. Do use it effectively to support and enhance your teaching and the children's learning.

- ❍ Use a calm, quiet voice rather than shouting.
- ❍ Praise children when they use their voices in a calm manner.
- ❍ Vary the tone and pitch of your voice while speaking to keep children listening, varying the levels, volumes and speeds at which you speak.
- ❍ Speak only when all of the children are listening. Talking over the children damages the voice and gives the wrong message to the children about speaking and listening.
- ❍ Use 'the tip of the tongue, the teeth and the lips' to model how to speak and how to use the whole mouth to form words and sounds.
- ❍ Use a very low, quiet voice to encourage the children to listen and draw them in.
- ❍ Use a variety of voices; for example:
  - – the *urgent* voice for gaining attention.
  - – the *happy* voice for praising a child.
  - – the *slow* voice for giving instructions.
  - – the *magic* voice for special moments.
- ❍ Use your mouth to express your feelings without saying anything, e.g. a gasp, a quick intake of breath, a breath out to represent shock or surprise.

L I S T 49   **Eye, eye!**

We have considered how to use our face and voice in managing behaviour but how do we use our eyes?

Your eyes:

○ Always make eye contact with the child and avoid standing above them; move down to their eye-level.

○ Use a wink to show you are pleased.

○ Use a stare to stop inappropriate behaviour.

○ Show children you are pleased with their behaviour by giving them a reassuring look.

○ Use your eyes when you talk; how wide or narrow they are can say many things.

○ Look at the children's eyes throughout the day as their mood and state of mind can often be detected in their eyes.

Their eyes:

○ Be aware that lowering the eyes is a sign of respect in some cultures – some children may not meet your gaze; remember this before you say 'Look at me when I'm talking to you'.

○ Tired eyes make for tired children who can get grumpy and moody; take this into consideration when planning for group work.

Helpful hands and arms

Your hands and arms can be used very effectively in encouraging children to be well behaved without you having to say a single word!

- Fold your arms and wait!
- Hold your hand out upright for the children to see – 'Stop!'
- Hold your arm in the air and encourage children to follow.
- Clap a rhythm for children to copy.
- Hold your fingers in the air and then lower each digit – 10, 9, 8, 7 . . .
- Place the side of your hand on your forehead like a pirate and 'look out' for good behaviour.
- Place fingers on lips.
- Make a 'telescope' with your hand and 'spy' well-behaved children.
- Say rhymes which involve hand movements, e.g. Two Little Dickie Birds. Sing songs and jingles, e.g. Hand Jive.
- Let children take their fingers for a 'walk' over their bodies.
- Click fingers and point towards a child to gain attention.
- Place hands on hips, to indicate disappointment.
- Tap your finger on your watch.

LIST 51 Perfect posture

We give many clues about the way we are feeling by the way we sit, stand and walk. Having the right posture can be the key to confidence in the classroom.

○ Stand straight and tall – if you look confident, the children will believe you are and will respond positively to you.

○ Slouching is a sign of apathy – it gives children the wrong message.

○ If you slouch, the children will slouch and they will have a poor attitude to their work.

○ Having a good posture means that you breathe well and remain relaxed. Breathing well means you can support your voice more effectively.

○ Supporting your voice means you can communicate more clearly.

○ Even when you are sitting sit with a straight back.

○ Walk tall and gracefully, giving the children the feeling that you are calm and relaxed. It will enable them to feel calm and relaxed.

○ Use your posture to punctuate what you are saying, shifting your weight, leaning in to tell a secret, etc.

Body and positioning

Where we position ourselves when we teach is very important, to ensure we are fully inclusive with our children and that we can maintain good eye contact with them.

○ When you stand in front of a seated class, your view is a 45-degree angle of the children. Those on the periphery are often excluded, so do regularly change the position you stand in.

○ Before you start, move children to a place where you can see them and they can see you.

○ Be aware of the distance you stand from the children – what message does it give? How much can you see of them? How much can they see of you?

○ Move from place to place as you teach so that the children remain 'awake' and enthusiastic.

○ Use a variety of levels for your teaching exposition – this will help to maintain the children's interest.

○ Try to avoid talking as you write on the board.

○ When you are sitting with the children, try to sit on their level.

○ Address individual children on their level so that you are eye to eye – if they have to look up to you it can be threatening for children.

○ Position children in the role of teacher rather than yourself.

○ Ensure children get the opportunity to shift their positions during longer seated tasks by, for example, taking a break, singing a song, standing up and walking around the classroom to music for a minute or two.

L I S T 53   Clothing considerations

It is said that clothes 'maketh the wo/man'; teachers need to think carefully about their clothing to ensure it is practical yet suitable for the classroom. Clothing can be a very powerful way to manage children's behaviour.

- Children who see teachers in smart clothing are more likely to respect and behave for them.
- Dress to suit the age and maturity of the children.
- Clothing should be clean, tidy and presentable.
- Make sure clothes are comfortable.
- Wear smart shoes which are comfortable to wear – avoid stilettos or fashionable trainers where possible.
- Ensure your clothing is appropriate for the activity – if the children are doing PE then you should be appropriately dressed. After PE you should find an appropriate time to change back into your clothing.
- Leave facial jewellery and hats at home where possible.
- Avoid clothing which is too short, skimpy or revealing.
- Avoid clothing which presents a health and safety risk.
- Avoid clothing with derogatory language or pictures.
- Avoid clothing with alcohol, drug, violent or sexual connotations.
- Avoid clothing which is see-through, ripped, torn, stained or smelly.
- Avoid wearing expensive clothing as it may get damaged. It is not the child's fault if it cost a lot!

Passing comments: children and their thoughts

Children's minds work in mysterious ways. Children can make us howl with laughter with passing comments which come out of their mouths without them thinking. Here are some wonderful little gems:

Child 1: Look! A badger! There! Quick – go tell Miss!
Child 2: No, don't do that! She'll only make us write about it!

Two children are arguing about their 'roles' in the home corner.
Child 1: Why should you be the mum? I've got bigger boobs than you!

Two five-year-old children are looking at an old TV guide.
Child 1: Did you see *that* on telly? It was rubbish! There was no plot!

Two four-year-old children are playing snap with a pack of cards. *Child 1 to Child 2*: If *you* don't let *me* win *I'll* tell *my* dad and *he'll* tell *your* dad and *he'll* tell *you* to let *me* win so let's cut out the middle man shall we?

Two children are talking about their teacher. *Child 1*: I love Mrs Jarvis! *Child 2*: Ummmm. My mum says she is just like her hair: disorganized!

Child to his friend: Do you like Miss Shaw, 'cause my dad would love to give her one!

Behaviour-Management Systems

 Making 'em feel good: motivational strategies and incentives

Motivating children helps them to achieve their potential. Positive recognition of a child's behaviour boosts self-esteem, helps children to choose appropriate behaviours and supports a positive atmosphere in the classroom.

- ○ Praise a child when they behave well. Do it often and with enthusiasm!
- ○ Use non-verbal strategies, e.g. a wink, a nod, a smile, thumbs up, a clap.
- ○ Mark children's work as they work, giving oral and written positive feedback.
- ○ Give out stickers, stamps and team points.
- ○ Ensure the child's name is clearly visible on the behaviour management displays in the classroom.
- ○ Use special privileges, e.g. sitting on a chair next to the teacher, being first in the line, calling out the names on the register, being 'special person' of the day, wearing the 'behaviour wrist band', talking to other classes about their good behaviour.
- ○ Use whole-class incentives, e.g. extra playtime, computer, golden time, choice of TV programme, playing children's CDs in class.
- ○ Write a note or make a phone call to parents.
- ○ Use behaviour awards, certificates, medals, hats, sashes and/or badges.
- ○ Display behaviour awards and good work on the class 'gallery board'.

L I S T 5 6   Suitable sanctions

Children need to know that there are consequences for their actions if they misbehave. Sanctions can be used effectively to manage inappropriate behaviour if they are age-appropriate and 'fit the crime'.

○ Use a warning system before you use sanctions.
○ Be consistent – have a progressive system so the sanction matches the severity of the behaviour.
○ Talk to children about sanctions they would/would not like to have.
○ Ensure the sanction is something the child does not like, e.g. a loss of privileges, last to leave the class, tidying the classroom, working on their own.
○ Do not use PE as a sanction – no child should be exempt from PE.
○ Choose sanctions which are convenient to you. If you make a child stay in at dinner time you should be able to monitor their behaviour during this time.
○ Never use sanctions which humiliate or cause physical pain.
○ Use time out.
○ Keep to time limits.
○ Send the child to another class with a 'behaviour' note.
○ Write to or call parents/carers if the behaviour continues.

**Targeting behaviour: target
statements**

Setting behaviour targets can be difficult; achieving these targets can
be even harder. Try some of the following tips for successful
behaviour target setting:

○ Always set behaviour targets with children. Ask them which
  areas they feel they would like to improve and make that the
  starting point.
○ Make targets simple and short – the child needs to be able to
  remember them.
○ Set one or two targets to start with.
○ Give all targets a 'short life' so that the child can be rewarded
  quickly for improvement.
○ Phrase targets so that the child fully understands the expectation.
  Ask the child to phrase the target as that way you are more likely
  to know that they understand.
○ Targets can be displayed in a number of ways:
  – on charts
  – on desks
  – on cards
  – on book marks
  – in the place where the behaviour occurs
  – in a book
○ Targets should be in places that are accessible to the child.
○ Achievements should be rewarded immediately.
○ Review targets regularly with the child, discuss progress and
  adjust and adapt targets as and when necessary.
○ Keep your expectations high; children will rise to meet them.

LIST 58 Using circle time

Circle time is a wonderful tool which can be used effectively to manage and prevent inappropriate behaviours in your classroom. For it to work, teachers need to plan for its use and ensure it regularly takes place.

○ Play warm-up games which develop team spirit, turn-taking, sharing and behaviour.

○ Use rounds to talk about behaviours, e.g. 'I like it when … ', 'I do not like it when … '

○ Use the main phase of circle time directly to address behaviour issues in the class.

○ Ask the children what is bothering them, and make this your starting point.

○ Use puppets to explore behaviours in a non-threatening environment.

○ Use masks to allow shy children to express their thoughts and feelings.

○ Use music to explore feelings and emotions.

○ Ensure children are taught not to mention children's names when they talk about incidents.

○ During circle time, teach children strategies to deal with inappropriate behaviour through role-play.

○ Ensure the closing phase brings the children together in a calming and positive way.

Charting behaviour

Behaviour charts should be a visual feature of every classroom. Children should be actively encouraged to feel proud of seeing good behaviour displayed in their classroom. Here are some suggestions as to how to chart behaviour:

○ *The Behaviour Tree* – add leaves and fruit when good behaviour occurs.

○ *The Flower* – add petals and colours.

○ *The Sea* – add starfish when the children have been 'little stars'.

○ *WOW cards* – these should be big and bright and given to a child when they 'WOW' you with their good behaviour.

○ *The Dartboard* – stick arrows on the different rings aiming for that ultimate bull's-eye!

○ *Mr Happy* – have a picture of Mr Happy (by Roger Hargreaves) or better still the toy and give him to children to look after when they have behaved beautifully.

○ *Rocket to the Moon!* – place a rocket on the earth and move the rocket closer to the moon as behaviour improves.

○ *Incy Wincy Spider* – can you get your spider up the drainpipe?

○ *This Is The Way We* ... (to the tune of 'Here We Go Round The Mulberry Bush') play together ... hang our coats ... tidy up ... Display the behaviour you are targeting that week or day and sing the song throughout the day.

○ *Whole-class jigsaw* – cut up a large picture/photograph of the whole class. When the last piece is added to the jigsaw when individuals have been well behaved, then all of the class receive a treat.

LIST 60   Valuing displays

The environment our children work and play in has a massive impact on their behaviour. Because of this, we need to consider what we put on walls, doors, windows and ceilings; it could make a difference!

❍ Ensure that all displays are beautifully presented.
❍ Use interactive displays which the children use daily.
❍ Create a star wall and have stars hanging from the ceiling.
❍ Use a 'bubble behaviour board' where well-behaved children can have their names floating in bubbles.
❍ Have a board full of smiley faces.
❍ Build a peacock tail, where colourful handprints are added for good behaviour.
❍ Encourage children to suggest class members they would like to see on the 'behaviour display'.
❍ Always ask children to explain why a child's name should go on the display.
❍ Have a behaviour board for parents and midday supervisors. Put on photos of children who have behaved well.
❍ Encourage children to talk to their parents about why they are on the board.
❍ Ask the children what they would like to see as their next behaviour display.
❍ Involve children in developing behaviour displays.
❍ Encourage children to use, refer to and discuss behaviour displays.
❍ Frequently add to and change displays.

LIST 61 Written evidence

Keeping written evidence of the behaviours you see in your class helps to monitor the children involved and how frequent and severe these behaviours are. We can then select the most appropriate management strategies for the specific behaviours and children.

- ○ Please do not log children's names and humiliate them at the same time – this is a private record-keeping system.
- ○ Use a recording system which is easy to use and keep, and is accessible to all who use it.
- ○ Ensure you have a clear key. Use coloured dots, percentages, symbols, ticks and crosses, scores out of ten, letters of the alphabet and/or numbers for speed of recording.
- ○ Respond to set questions or statements to reflect on behaviours seen.
- ○ Ensure any proformas you use have adequate space for written comments.
- ○ Make notes on sticky notes or labels.
- ○ Complete action notes on your weekly or daily planning sheets.
- ○ Fill in behaviour books.
- ○ Log your evidence as soon as you possibly can.
- ○ Monitor behaviour in school profiles.
- ○ Use school tracking systems to log information.

L I S T 62 Celebrating success

Good behaviour should be celebrated; if success is acknowledged it is more likely to continue. Celebrate success simply by looking at a child who has behaved well, and:

○ smile
○ wink
○ give the thumbs up
○ verbally give praise.

Ask the other children to do the same:

○ give a round of applause
○ give three cheers
○ play 'We are the champions' by Queen
○ say 'thank you'.

Also celebrate success by:

○ using sticker charts. Keep these at school and/or send them home.
○ putting a marble in the jar. When the jar is full enjoy a treat.
○ having a 'star of the week'. Talk to that child about why they are star of the week.
○ using circle time to praise children and focus on appropriate/good behaviour.
○ sending stars/certificates/a special soft toy home at the end of the week with a child who has behaved well. This encourages children to share their success with people at home.
○ sharing positive behaviour with parents and not just the negative. Use assemblies and parents' meetings to achieve this.

LIST 63   Involving parents and carers

All parents and carers want the best for their children. Informing and involving parents and carers in managing their child's behaviour helps them to feel like a valuable part of their child's education.

○ As soon as behaviour becomes a concern, act on it.
○ Always be honest about the child's behaviour.
○ Show parents and carers any appropriate written evidence you have.
○ Inform parents and carers of what you are doing about the behaviour in school.
○ Always listen carefully to what parents and carers have to say.
○ Discuss and identify possible causes for the behaviours seen.
○ Ensure that parents and carers understand that you need to work together.
○ Allow parents and carers to offer suggestions to manage their child's behaviour.
○ Establish a clear plan of action, with specific targets, for managing the child's behaviour at home and school. Make sure everyone is happy with this.
○ Ensure parents and carers know you are confident that their child's behaviour will improve.
○ Keep parents and carers up to date with any changes in their child's behaviour.
○ Encourage parents and carers to update you on the child's behaviour at home. Consider effective ways of doing this, e.g. a letter or note, spoken word, or a behaviour card.
○ Plan dates to review progress.
○ Always generously thank parents and carers for their efforts.

LIST 64

Parents and *their* behaviour

We deal with parents (and carers) daily and they are an important part of our working lives. Just like children, *their* behaviours and personalities differ. We need to be aware of these behaviours so that we can manage them appropriately. Here are some parent 'types' and some appropriate strategies:

- The *fussing* parent: Promote the child's independence by asking them to hang their own coat up, etc. in front of their parent.
- The *worried* parent: Explain to them that there are no problems and if necessary phone them later in the day to reassure them.
- The *aggressive* parent: Avoid being confrontational. Be firm and polite and don't hesitate to involve the headteacher if their behaviour is inappropriate or threatening.
- The *pushy* parent: Listen to how wonderful and intelligent they believe their child to be, but avoid their views influencing your own assessment.
- The *invisible* parent: If you find it difficult to catch some parents, leave messages on answer phones or send letters home.
- The *negative* parent: Constantly praise the child in front of this parent. They need to know that their child has good qualities as well as the not so good.
- The *talented* parent: Harness their skills – can they sew costumes? Hear readers? Help with gardening? Use them!

Involving the community

Children need to be taught to be well behaved not only in school, but also outside of school. Poor behaviour can affect the local area and community if children believe they can behave inappropriately. Using people in the community can help children to see that good behaviour needs to be used all of the time.

- ○ Ask the local constabulary to talk to the children about behaviours they like to see, particularly linked to road safety. Allow them to tell suitable stories which get children to question the behaviours of people the police come into contact with.
- ○ Ask people from local shops and businesses to come and work with children, promoting behaviours they like to see in their place of work.
- ○ Encourage the local vicar and members of other religions to deliver whole-school assemblies, using stories from holy texts to encourage good behaviour.
- ○ Invite members of the local council to talk and work with children on projects to develop a nicer community and local area. Allow children to reflect on the behaviours of people who have covered walls in graffiti or destroyed playground areas.
- ○ Invite different members of the community into school, e.g. the elderly, the disabled and ethnic minorities so that children can demonstrate positive behaviours associated with politeness and acceptance of others.
- ○ Go on visits and trips in the local area so that children are able to model their good behaviours.

Behaviour through the Day | 8

LIST 66 — Making an entrance

Behaviour management begins the very moment you collect your class from the playground. Establishing a smooth transition from the playground to the cloakroom, and then into the classroom is essential in getting the day off to a good start.

- Stand in the playground five minutes before school starts, so that parents can talk to you or arrange to see you at the end of the day if necessary.
- Only allow children into school if they are in a straight, quiet line.
- Use chants to gain attention, e.g. 'Are we ready?' *'YES WE ARE!'*
- Remind children of your expectations *before* they move.
- Get children to enter school in different ways, e.g. roll feet from heel to toe, tip-toe, walk on heels, like a soldier, like penguins, like fish fingers (a personal favourite), side-stepping.
- Be on the look out for good behaviour, and acknowledge it as the children move.
- Position children along the corridor and near to the cloakroom to monitor noise levels.
- Set a time limit to get into class from the cloakroom using a stop-watch or a sand timer.

Calm in the cloakroom

The cloakroom can soon become a place for silliness, arguments, stealing and time wasting. Setting up routines and expectations can keep it cool and calm.

- ❑ Involve the children in making the rules so they have ownership of them.
- ❑ Make it their space so they take responsibility for it.
- ❑ Give the children jobs within the cloakroom so that it is a purposeful space.
- ❑ Make sure everybody has a peg to hang their coat and bag, which is clearly labelled with their name.
- ❑ Ensure the coat pegs are the right height for the children.
- ❑ Have a box for fallen items to keep the floor clear and prevent accidents.
- ❑ Play calm and gentle music in the cloakroom to instil the right mood.
- ❑ Sing a song as part of your morning routine that starts in the playground and finishes as the children sit down in class.
- ❑ Have cloakroom attendants.
- ❑ Have small groups of children collect their coats to prevent accidents and high noise levels.
- ❑ Encourage children to leave their valuables at home or give them to you for safekeeping. Always ask children to bring dinner money into the classroom at the start of the day.
- ❑ Monitor children walking in and out of the cloakroom to prevent them running and sliding in the area.

The 'magic carpet': carpet time

Carpet time is a lovely opportunity to come together and have time
away from desks and other classroom activities. Try some of the
following ideas to ensure you have a 'magical' time:

○ Give children their own special space to sit in.
○ Have mats/carpet samples/cushions for children to sit on, as it
  helps them to stay where they should be.
○ Unless otherwise asked, have a 'hands and feet to yourself' rule.
○ Display rules for carpet time near to the carpet area and ask the
  children to remind you of what they are before commencing with
  the activity.
○ Try to have rules that can be demonstrated through gestures:
  fingers on lips for quiet, cupping ears for listening, pointing to
  your head for thinking.
○ Keep the carpet activity interactive so everybody is involved and
  interested. This does not mean that carpet time cannot be
  peaceful; you may be asking the children to think, imagine, read,
  etc.
○ Vary the activities during carpet time so that you avoid
  predictability and boredom.
○ Sit with the children or sit on a low chair or beanbag.
○ Ensure smaller children sit at the front. If they cannot see over
  taller children they are more likely to misbehave.

LIST 69 Moving up and down and all around

Moving around the classroom can be a time for inappropriate behaviour. Using different strategies for moving from the carpet to desks, and from activity to activity can help to make transitions smooth and fun.

○ Play a piece of music with a regular beat and move to it in time.

○ Encourage the children to count down with you from ten to zero. 'Blast off!' denotes the start of the activity.

○ Ask the children to move from place to place in character. This could be related to a book you are reading. Each time you move around choose a new character.

○ Move around exploring moods – happily, dreamily, slowly, etc. This can be linked to music.

○ Hold up signs so the children focus on you. This is also a good non-verbal strategy and can encourage children to move quietly.

○ Move around in 'follow my leader' fashion.

○ Sing your favourite class song as you move.

○ Clap a beat and ask the children to copy it as they move; it encourages the children to focus their listening and attention and avoid chatter.

LIST 70 Go for it! Free play

Free play is an important and essential feature of young children's learning. It allows exploration of behaviours both appropriate and inappropriate. Manage and improve behaviour during free play by:

○ Structuring free play by providing children with appropriate and limited resources.
○ Controlling the number of children in play areas by putting up signs they have made, providing the appropriate number of aprons and matching the number of tags to the number of children. Teach children strategies to manage this themselves.
○ Providing an appropriate range of free play equipment, e.g. building equipment, small world play, tactile play, etc.
○ Providing some focused, calming, quiet activities, books to read, tracing activities, etc.
○ Sending children who have been behaving inappropriately to 'quieter' activities to provide opportunities for them to calm down.
○ Talking to children about the play equipment available before they begin their activities. Discuss appropriate behaviour and expectations.
○ Giving children a time limit and remind them when there are five/three minutes to go before they must stop.
○ Stopping children occasionally to praise the behaviour and allow individuals to model appropriate behaviour for others.

LIST 71 Choices: independent activities

Promoting independence is an important aspect of education, although providing too much can lead to behaviour problems. We need to train and manage children appropriately to prevent this from happening.

- ○ Write the rules for independent play together using words and pictures.
- ○ Place the rules where everyone can see them.
- ○ Encourage children to explain to individuals who are behaving inappropriately exactly how they should be behaving. To begin with you will need to model how to do this! And practise how to do this! And reinforce how to do this! And praise children who do this well!
- ○ Model an activity first by making it adult-led, before allowing children to do it independently.
- ○ Put systems in place for children to use if they need help when working independently.
- ○ Encourage children to refer to boards or information in the classroom which may help them.
- ○ Make signs, e.g. 'We are working by ourselves', for the children to put at their independent activities to remind them to solve problems themselves.

LIST 72 Being fabulous during PE

PE can be a stressful time, with children moving about with the potential to hurt themselves and others if they do not behave appropriately. It is essential to have clear rules, routines and effective management strategies to encourage good behaviour and prevent accidents.

- You *must not* use PE as a sanction for children's poor behaviour – every child has the right to physical activity.
- Talk about the health and safety issues before children enter the hall.
- Remind children of the rules.
- Only allow children to start activities when they are quiet and attentive.
- Only blow the whistle in an emergency – if children hear the whistle all of the time they will soon stop responding to it.
- Use time out from an activity for a small period of time if children present themselves as a health and safety issue.
- Always keep your back to the wall and scan the room.
- Use children to demonstrate actions and skills.
- Play music quietly as children work to keep noise levels down.
- Ensure there is more 'doing' and less 'talking'.
- Allow children moments of rest.

L I S T 73 **Being happy in the hall**

For young children, the hall is a wide-open space which must be explored. In some cases, 'exploring' often means running wildly around the hall!

- ○ Before leaving the classroom talk to the children about appropriate hall behaviour.
- ○ Make the rules clear and state what WILL happen if they do not behave appropriately.
- ○ Walk to the hall in a quiet, calm line.
- ○ Stand quietly outside the hall before entering.
- ○ Take out 'loud voices' and take off 'fast feet'.
- ○ Model how to move into the hall and ask the children to follow.
- ○ Model how to sit in the hall.
- ○ If an individual behaves inappropriately ask them to sit to the side.
- ○ Only ask children at the side to join in the activity when they are calm and have some understanding of why they were removed.
- ○ Stop the children and ask them to watch one child who is an excellent role model of how to move around/sit/talk in the hall.
- ○ Some children are frightened by the hall and large spaces. Give them a partner to make them feel secure.

Being splendid during snack time

Snack time should be quiet and well managed to avoid spillages and silliness. Whether the children have their snack inside or outside the classroom, ensure you always follow the same routine to help the children to remember what is expected of them.

If you are inside:

○ Ask everybody to sit down in their space on the carpet.
○ Ask a child to give out the snack when everybody is sitting down.
○ If children have brought their own snacks send them in small groups to get them.
○ Play music while snack is eaten or read a story/poem to the children.
○ Have a special snack time reward system to reinforce good behaviour.

If you are outside:

○ If it is still appropriate, sit down. Turn it into a picnic with a large blanket!
○ If snack is during playtime, encourage the children to eat their snack before playing boisterous games.
○ Use the same reward system as you had for inside.
○ Have children and other adults to look out for good behaviour and give out rewards.

L I S T 7 5 Snacks and slurps

Lunchtime can be 'an experience' – noisy children, some behaving inappropriately, all in the same place at the same time! To try and make the whole experience calmer here are some suggestions:

❍ Wait quietly outside the dinner hall so that everyone is calm and quiet before they enter.

❍ Play calming music to set the mood for dining.

❍ Model how to move around the dinner hall.

❍ Occasionally join the children to eat.

❍ Model how to sit.

❍ Model how to eat appropriately.

❍ Model how to have a polite conversation between mouthfuls.

❍ Avoid movement around the hall by having lots of bins to put rubbish in, and encourage children to keep their rubbish in their lunch box until they have finished.

❍ Encourage talking to your neighbour instead of shouting across the dinner table.

❍ Encourage children to wait patiently and put their hand up if they need help.

❍ Train midday supervisors to promote acceptable behaviour and discourage unacceptable behaviour.

❍ Encourage children to respect midday supervisors.

❍ Encourage children to leave the hall in the quiet, calm and sensible manner in which they arrived.

❍ Use stickers to reward appropriate lunchtime behaviour.

LIST 76 Being super during story time

Story time should be fun, exciting and captivating for children.
Remember that it does not always have to be done at the end of the
day. Using storytelling skills and these little tips will make for
smooth story time.

- Create the right atmosphere, e.g. dim the lights, play soft music
  in the background, maybe even have some candles lit around the
  room.
- Set clear ground rules about behaviour before you start.
- Try to tell the story without referring to the book – tell stories
  you love.
- Use visual aids to keep the children's interest, e.g. puppets,
  masks and costumes.
- Vary the tone and volume of your voice for characters.
- Use actions and movement to maintain children's interest.
- Ask children to close their eyes and 'paint pictures' in their heads
  of the story they hear.
- Involve the children, e.g. use repetitive phrases, create sound
  effects with their mouths and bodies. Ask them questions to
  assess whether they were listening and understood what the story
  was about.
- Use well-behaved children to mime parts of the story as you tell
  it.
- Allow children to tell their own stories to the class.
- Be flexible with story time – change it occasionally to poetry
  time, song time, drama time, etc.

Do the children leave the classroom *in spite of you* rather than *because of you*? At the end of the school day children are tired and ready to go home, but how can we make their exit more fun and orderly?

○ Have a song playing at the end of the day, or that the children sing, as they collect their coats and bags from the cloakroom.

○ Send the children out in small groups based on the month of their birthday, the colour of their socks or eyes, for example.

○ Lead the children out in a 'Ministry of Funny Walks' fashion.

○ If you have children who clash with each other, always ensure you send one out first and the other last to avoid conflict. Vary who goes out first!

○ Send children out to chants and rhymes.

○ Ask children to tell you one thing they have learned during the course of the day before going home.

○ Use 'sitting chains' – choose a child who is sitting nicely to go first, ask them to choose the next person and so on.

○ Encourage children to try and creep past you without you hearing them.

○ Leave the room in different ways, e.g. like a penguin, like a movie star, like a kite, etc.

Behaviour-Management Strategies

9

LIST 78   Using visual aids

Visual aids are an effective way to manage children's behaviour, particularly if they are bright and colourful, simple to use by both the teacher and the children, and acknowledge good behaviour. Children will only respond to them if they know how they work and are used regularly and consistently by the teacher. Consider using some of the following:

○ Smiley/sad face cards.
○ Sun and Cloud – place names in them to indicate good/not so good behaviour.
○ Referee cards – show the yellow card as a warning and the red card as time out.
○ Stop sign – hold it up to gain control of individuals, groups and the whole class.
○ Good behaviour stickers and stamps.
○ Individual and group behaviour cards.
○ Puppets that 'look' for good behaviour.
○ Coloured papers – show different colours which indicate how teachers/children are feeling, e.g. red for angry, blue for sad, yellow for happy.
○ Sand timer – indicates the time children may lose from golden time.
○ Picture-perfect behaviour – photographs of the children modelling good behaviour are shown to guide those in need of a little support!
○ Facial expression masks – paper plate masks are held to the teacher's face to indicate feelings about children's behaviour.

L I S T 79   Using praise to motivate

If we stay positive and offer praise to our children they are much more likely to be motivated and want to achieve. This will inevitably make our job easier and our days much more pleasant. We can use *non-verbal* praise through:

- ○ eye contact, e.g. winking
- ○ smiling
- ○ giving the thumbs up
- ○ a gentle pat on the back or a squeeze of a shoulder
- ○ encouraging the children to do all of the above with each other.

We can give *verbal* praise through phrases such as:

- ○ 'I am really glad you are in my class because ... '
- ○ 'Today you are my star person because ... '
- ○ 'I am so proud of you because ... '
- ○ 'Your Mum/Dad will be so proud of you because ... '
- ○ 'I want you to sit next to me because ... '
- ○ 'I want you at the front of my line because ... '
- ○ 'You are going on the smiley board because ... '
- ○ 'You can wear the happy badge today because ... '
- ○ 'You are fantastic because ... '
- ○ 'You can get a sticker because ... '
- ○ 'You can be the first to go out to play because ... '
- ○ 'You can choose which book to read today because ... '

Using rewards

Rewards are very motivating for children – they boost self-esteem, give a great deal of satisfaction and raise engagement and commitment levels towards learning in the classroom.

- ○ Ensure rewards 'fit' the behaviour, are age-appropriate and are publicly and privately given.
- ○ Reward the *behaviour* and not the *child*.
- ○ Use a range of individual, group, class and school rewards.
- ○ Use praise, tokens, credits, stickers, stamps, badges, written comments, ticks and/or smiley faces to reward individuals.
- ○ Use team points, certificates, stickers, prizes, plaques and trophies to reward groups of children or classes.
- ○ Children love privileges, e.g. use of school equipment, mentions in assemblies and being given extra responsibilities, e.g. special person of the day, monitors. Use them where appropriate.
- ○ Ask children how they would like to be rewarded.
- ○ If you use marks, grades, comments and stars on the children's work, let the children actually look at them!
- ○ Ensure you share out your rewards equally and fairly between the lower, middle and higher ability children – fair's fair!
- ○ Remember: any rewards given for good behaviour cannot be taken away later on in the day.

LIST 81 Using criticism

Nobody likes to be criticized as it takes away confidence and leaves feelings of resentment. Make criticism a positive, constructive learning experience by doing it sensibly and sensitively.

❍ Ask children to tell you what they could have done better, and how they could achieve this.

❍ Praise them for recognizing things they have done wrong.

❍ Give them the opportunity to make decisions for themselves about how to put things right.

❍ Have systems for recognizing the good and improving the not so good, e.g. two stars and a wish; apples and worms; sunshine and clouds.

❍ Be honest about the mistakes you make to help the children to realize that mistakes are okay and that you can learn from them.

❍ Take responsibility for things children get wrong, e.g. 'I'm sorry, I don't think I explained that properly to you . . . ', 'Was that my fault for not reminding us of the rules . . . ?' Say sorry if you do make a mistake.

❍ Use criticism as little as possible and always ensure you 'sandwich' it between positive comments.

❍ Reward the children when they act on comments for improvement.

❍ When a child has behaved badly, tell them how it affects others and give them time to reflect on this.

❍ Tell children when they are doing the right thing; they know how it feels inside when they have made a bad choice – help children to recognize the feelings of making the right choices too.

LIST 82 Using intervention

Some teachers believe that children should manage their own behaviour as it is believed to support child development, promote independence and demonstrate that children do not always need an adult referee to sort out their problems. However, most teachers use intervention strategies to manage behavioural issues in their class, to prevent incidents getting out of control. Here is some advice surrounding intervention:

○ Using your voice is only one way to intervene. Consider using hand signals, facial and body language or sounds.

○ Try to intervene sooner rather than later, otherwise things might get a little messy!

○ Use the 'three-second stop gap' before you intervene – assess the situation before you intervene, ensuring you know who is involved, what is actually happening and why it is happening.

○ Try to keep your interventions short and to the point – if you talk at the children for too long they will soon stop listening to you.

○ Approach the children calmly and use a soft voice so as not to disrupt other children in the classroom.

○ Ensure you have the attention of all of the children involved when you use intervention.

○ After intervening, keep a close eye on the children involved to assess the effectiveness of your approach.

L I S T 8 3   Using peer and self intervention

Children learn quickly from one another. Allow opportunities for children to work alongside each other to gain a better understanding of behaving well.

- ❍ 'Behaviour buddies' – pair up children who sometimes 'forget' the rules with those who adhere well to them.
- ❍ Befriending – this is essentially about building on the natural helping skills which children learn through everyday interactions with friends and family.
- ❍ Create opportunities for dialogue between children, to talk about good behaviour and the effects of poor behaviour on others.
- ❍ Allow plenty of thinking time. Once a situation has occurred, give children the opportunity to sit quietly and reflect on their actions.
- ❍ Peer mediation. This is based on a 'no-blame' attitude, finding a win-win situation with no punishment linked. This helps children to solve their problems and to explore outcomes in which all parties are happy.
- ❍ In the classroom always identify those behaving well, explain why their behaviour is desirable and try to turn a blind eye to poor behaviour.

LIST 84   Using stories and role-play

Stories and role-play are excellent vehicles for encouraging, exploring and demonstrating good behaviour. By exploring feelings and emotions in a safe and secure environment, children can develop their own understanding of how to behave.

❍ Modify events in stories, ensuring characters have strategies for dealing with situations which children can transfer into their own experiences.

❍ Use traditional stories which allow children to see the effect that inappropriate behaviour has on others.

❍ Encourage children to think about issues from the perspective of others by hot-seating characters.

❍ Create caring and collaborative situations in the role-play area, e.g. taking care of plants/babies/animals.

❍ Use finger/hand puppets to explore how to make 'Melvin the Frog' feel better.

❍ Develop sharing skills with a 'prop bag' that has a variety of things in it that need sharing, i.e. flowers, stickers, etc.

❍ Use tag systems that encourage independence, self-discipline and turn-taking in the role-play area.

❍ Use freeze-frame scenes from stories to depict a mood or feeling.

❍ Telephone talk – talk to children 'on the telephone' about how you are feeling about an incident which has just happened.

Using questions and answers

How often do we examine what we say to children when they have behaved inappropriately? Are you sometimes embarrassed/shocked when you hear other adults reprimanding children? Using simple questions can help children to think about their behaviour.

○ When you ask a child about an incident, listen carefully to the response.

○ Ask why the child did what they did.

○ Again, listen carefully; sometimes we might not be questioning the culprit!

○ Ask children how they would feel if someone called them a name or hurt them, etc.

○ Ask children what they can do to put it right, and then let them put it right!

○ Ask them what they will do in the future.

○ For repeated poor behaviour, give children a choice – they can either continue with that behaviour but [a sanction] will happen, or they can stop now and get back on task. If necessary carry out the sanction, reminding them that they made the choice.

○ Tell children you are disappointed or saddened by their behaviour rather than being cross.

○ Let the children know how you feel when they behave badly, and ask them if they can tell you why you feel like that.

LIST 86 — Using sounds

Children can be so overwhelmed by noise levels and voices in the classroom that they soon 'stop listening'. Using sounds allows you to manage behaviour without having to say a word!

○ Shake a tambourine to gain the children's attention. Rainmakers, cymbals, bells and other instruments are alternatives to the tambourine.

○ Clap a simple clapping rhythm, encouraging the children to join in. Fold your arms when you want to stop the rhythm.

○ Use the number of 'tings' on a triangle to indicate a certain action, e.g. *one* ting asks the children to sit up straight, *two* tings asks the children to move.

○ Ring a little bell when you want the attention of the children or use it as a signal that the noise is getting too loud in class.

○ Play sound effects of applause and cheering on a tape recorder when you see good behaviour being used in class.

○ Place a metronome near to the child when they are having some 'time out'. The methodical ticking helps to focus the child's attention on a sound rather than the incident in which they were involved.

Music can be a very powerful tool in the fight against poor behaviour!

○ Associate music to an activity, e.g. the *Mission Impossible* theme music to tidy up time.

○ Play music in response to children's moods, e.g. a lullaby to calm them, the *1812 Overture* to liven them up!

○ Play quiet music when the children are working, to manage noise levels.

○ Play dance music to relieve restless children on the carpet – 'Get up and move!'

○ Play music by Mozart while the children are working; it has been proven that his music helps children to learn, particularly during mathematics.

○ Play favourite pop songs as a reward for good behaviour. Ask the children to bring in a CD or a tape of the songs. (Check for appropriate lyrics!)

○ Play music in response to how the children's behaviour is making *you* feel. Change the music if their behaviour changes your feelings. Allow children to select music in response to their own feelings.

○ Play different pieces of music to elicit different emotional responses. Encourage children to use this vocabulary when they are engaged in a confrontation as opposed to using physical action.

L I S T 88   Using quick-fire strategies

Once good behaviour has been demonstrated, it needs to be maintained. We can do this throughout the day by using some of the following quick-fire strategies:

❍ Smile directly at individual children to praise positive behaviour.
❍ Always say 'Thank you', and use phrases such as 'I like the way that you ... ', etc.
❍ 'Wiggle and jiggle' – keep children moving between activities to help them to concentrate and behave for longer.
❍ Give out lots of stickers.
❍ Ask all of the children to listen by putting their hands on their heads and looking directly at you. Always expect them to do this.
❍ Play 'follow my leader' – if you are wiggling your fingers, so should everyone else.
❍ Put hands on heads, shoulders, knees and toes, and then listen!
❍ Always make eye contact.
❍ Stop all the children to highlight and praise the positive behaviour of one child.
❍ Sit the 'little rascal' next to you or near your feet so you can keep a close eye on them.
❍ Gently touch them on the shoulder if they are behaving inappropriately. This allows you to continue to teach while managing behaviour.
❍ Have a 'smiley board'. Add names of children who have made you smile during the day.

Giving children strategies to deal with their own behaviour enables them to take responsibility for their actions. 'Time out' is one way that children can learn to reflect on how they have behaved, or it can be used to prevent an undesirable outburst.

○ 'Time out' should not be perceived as a punishment.

○ Make the 'time out' area comfortable for children.

○ Allow children to choose to go into the area when they feel the need to.

○ Display posters with positive pictures and statements in the area that provide 'food for thought'.

○ Provide books that have simple stories with values and moral messages.

○ Give the child a specific question or statement for reflection.

○ Remind children that the 'time out' area is for thinking and most importantly for positive change.

○ Ask the child to tell you what they can do to make things better now.

○ Give the child the opportunity to put it right.

○ Once the incident has been rectified, move on and show your pleasure in their choice.

LIST 90 **Using strategies for the twenty-first century**

As the need for more effective practical behaviour-management strategies continues, here are some new and innovative approaches being used to fight the 'behaviour battle':

○ Aromatherapy – use of candles and scents in the classroom.
○ Calming corners – cushions, magazines and music are set up in the classroom for children to chill out in.
○ Healthy eating – children are given fresh fruit every day.
○ Physical activity – PE sessions (football, step classes, aerobics, circuit training and running clubs) are taking place either before school or as the first lesson.
○ Aggression cushions – cushions are 'used' by children in an attempt to release their aggression.
○ Rest mats – children are given time during the school day to lie on their mats and relax/sleep.
○ Behaviour contracts – children discuss and sign contracts devised by staff, governors, parents and the children at school.
○ Playground games – midday supervisors are being encouraged to teach and play playground games with the children, and use equipment to control children's behaviour.
○ 'Playground peacemakers' – older children are encouraged to be a support mechanism for other children in the school.
○ 'Behaviour warriors' – children are nominated by children in the school to look out for good behaviour, praising and rewarding children on the spot.
○ Behaviour coordinators – teachers are now using tracking systems and observations to monitor behaviour throughout the school.

Behaviour and the 'Little Rascals'

The *aggressive* child

There are many reasons as to why a child will become physically or verbally aggressive in the classroom (refer to *Clarifying the causes*, p. 6). It is important to use strategies to support these children while ensuring their behaviour does not disturb or harm other children.

- When attracting the attention of the child, lower your voice and talk quietly.
- Avoid arguing with the child.
- Use clear and concise language to instruct the child.
- Avoid long drawn-out discussions – keep sentences short and to the point.
- Remind the child of the rules of the classroom – refer them to the display about rules in the classroom.
- Use time out, the thinking chair or thinking time to give the child time to calm down.
- Give the child two choices, e.g. 'Either choose a different toy to play with or sit with me for five minutes!'
- Catch the child being good later on in the day – praise them.
- Try to channel the child's aggression into a purposeful physical activity – running races, playing football, playing on the bikes.
- Remember it is the behaviour you are unhappy about, not the child.
- If the child is potentially a danger to themselves or others, as a last resort, physically restrain the child.

L I S T 9 2 The *lazy* child

Everyone has a child in their class who drives them to distraction because they are just so lazy, or they simply cannot be bothered! We need to find ways of encouraging these children and involving them in their own success.

○ Encourage them to help with tidying up by giving them a simple but specific task to complete.

○ Always check that they have completed the task and praise them when they have done so.

○ Gradually make the tidying-up task more involved and demanding to increase their level of responsibility and involvement.

○ Try giving them a partner to work/tidy up with. This will give them more incentive to become involved.

○ Always check that the child's partner is not doing ALL the work.

○ Always set the child achievable goals.

○ Ask the child to share their work with the rest of the class and let them know that this will be happening before they start the task.

○ Involve the child in physical activities and keep checking they are involved.

○ Repeatedly inform the child of how much longer they have to complete a task.

○ Don't give them opportunities to opt out, keep checking up on them with regular words of encouragement.

The *crying* child

There are a number of reasons why children cry in school, e.g. being separated from their parents, they have fallen over, they are being bullied, they feel sick or stressed. It is, however, important to manage this behaviour to calm the child and ensure they do not disrupt or upset other children in the classroom.

○ Offer reassurance through a kind word, a smile, a hand on the shoulder.

○ Have a 'tearful teddy' for children to hug when upset.

○ Have tissues to hand.

○ Distract children with 'special jobs' or creative learning and teaching.

○ Sit children on the 'special chair'.

○ Leave children for a while – give them some space to calm down in their own time.

○ Allow children to express their emotions, but do not let them become too distressed by them.

○ Use drama/role-play/small world resources to allow children to express their feelings.

○ Pair children up with a friend who can look after them for a while.

○ Plan something the child likes, e.g. PE, music.

○ Talk to the class about ways they could make each other feel better.

○ Use a teaching assistant or parent helper to offer support.

○ Praise children when they are calm.

○ Use 'bravery' stickers.

L I S T 9 4   The *friendless* child

A number of children are loners and by nature find it very difficult to make friends. It is our responsibility to help these children to socialize. The following ideas are suggestions as to how to do this:

○ Ask them to choose a friend to sit next to on the carpet.
○ Ask them to choose their favourite person with whom to read a book.
○ Ask them to choose whom they would like to play with.

All of the above will build self-esteem and will allow them to see that it is possible to have different friends.

○ Teach children how to talk to their friends.
○ Teach children to look for their friends if they want someone to play with/share a book.
○ Teach children how to share.
○ Encourage all children to have a range of friends and be willing to play with a range of children.
○ Encourage children to sit next to different people on the carpet.
○ Give children jobs, and encourage them to choose someone they would like to help them to complete the task.
○ Make yourself unavailable so that children have to find other children with whom to talk/play.

The *chatterbox* child

Everyone has met a 'chatterbox' – the child who goes on, and on, and *on*. Talk is a healthy and constructive element of early years education, but there are some children who need a little more 'direction'. We need to teach children when to talk, how to talk and that it is also important to listen.

❍ Teach children to think before they speak using 'thinking time'.
❍ Teach children to 'hold it in their heads' until it is the right time to talk.
❍ Use talking partners.
❍ Develop listening skills by asking the child to repeat back to you what has been said to them.
❍ During carpet and group activities, sit the child next to you so that you can help them.
❍ Play games that encourage children to listen to others as well as talk themselves. Praise children when they act appropriately.
❍ Sprinkle imaginary 'speaking and listening dust' over the children. Explain that this magic dust will help them to think about when to listen and when it is the right time to talk.
❍ Use 'listening' stickers.
❍ Use language positively.
❍ Model good speaking and listening skills.

LIST 96 The *clinging* child

Sometimes children find it difficult to be separated from their parent or carer, or to leave the side of an adult. This can become a problem and be detrimental to their social development. Encourage clingy children to come into the classroom and with little fuss separate from their parent/carer by:

○ smiling at them.
○ taking their hand.
○ explaining what time mum or dad will return.
○ encouraging them to give mum/dad one last big hug and then moving them away. Sometimes it may be appropriate to ask the parent/carer to give the child one last hug and then just leave.
○ distracting them with a book to share with friends.

Encourage clingy children to leave your/your teaching assistant's side by:

○ giving them a partner and asking them to look after their partner, as well as their partner looking after them.
○ explaining the activities available to them and encouraging them to choose one of them.
○ asking them to consider which activity they will visit next to prevent them from returning to your side.
○ encouraging the child to bring something in from home and to talk about it with another child in the class to build up their confidence.

LIST 97 The 'bullied' and the 'bully'

Both the 'bully' and the 'bullied' need strategies to manage their behaviour and feelings. The 'bully' is often insecure and unhappy and treats people unkindly to gain control. The 'bullied' is often a child that will not retaliate.

Supporting the 'bully':

○ Help the 'bully' to build their self-esteem by getting to know them; use their interests to build confidence.
○ Teach respect for themselves and for others.
○ Use circle time to talk about good qualities in people and highlight the 'bully's' good qualities.
○ Give the 'bully' a buddy for playtimes to draw them away from routine behaviour.
○ Encourage team games in the classroom and outside to unite the children at play.
○ As the 'bully' whether they would like to be bullied. Do *they* think it would be fun if it was done to them?

Supporting the 'bullied':

○ Teach the child strategies for walking away from the 'bully'.
○ Give the child a buddy who is confident and happy – the 'bullied' child will learn from their peer.
○ Build confidence in the child to tell a teacher.
○ Use role-play in the classroom to develop more strategies for dealing with bullies.

LIST 98 The *invisible* child

Some children are so quiet, shy and timid that they almost become invisible. Although these children very rarely cause us problems we need to be aware of them and accommodate them in our classrooms.

○ Regularly smile at them so that they know that they are included and not forgotten.
○ Sit them next to you so that you can gently persuade them to join in and then support them when they do.
○ Encourage them to join in with group and class discussions by asking them to repeat phrases after you. Gradually expect them to say more independently.
○ Let them play and work with small groups of children so that they feel more comfortable.
○ Give them a partner, ensuring the partner is not too loud and confident.
○ Allow them to choose the activities they would like to be involved in.
○ Create group singing sessions, and encourage them to join in as this will be less threatening than talking/singing individually.
○ Allow them 'quiet time' to opt out and sit quietly when they need to.
○ Ensure they do not always choose to distance themselves, by directing them to specific tasks with other children.

LIST 99

The *listening* child . . . *or are they*?

Ensuring every child is listening to you is certainly a challenge; you will always come across one child who does not appear to be paying attention. Try out these strategies to make the 'listener' listen!

○ Use your teacher stare!
○ Make a sound, e.g. click your fingers, play a musical instrument, clap your hands, whistle, hum.
○ Point to your eyes with your fingers while saying 'Look this way please!' or 'Focus!'
○ Ask the 'listener' a direct question.
○ Praise a child who *is* listening well.
○ Use listening stickers to entice children to listen.
○ Change your voice to attract attention, e.g. sing your next sentence, use silly voices, and alter the pitch, tone and volume of your delivery.
○ Move the 'listener' so they are directly in your eyesight.
○ Change your activity – if one child has stopped listening, others will soon begin to follow.
○ Use peers to check their partners are listening – look at them, ask them a question.
○ Practise strategic ignoring.
○ Say a silly word in mid-sentence to attract attention, e.g. 'I am *squigglehop* looking for smart sitters!'
○ Give the 'listener' something to do, e.g. hold the pointer, look for good listeners.

LIST 100 The *fiddling* child

Fiddle de dee-fiddle de doo. It can be very annoying, can't it? Velcro straps on shoes, tapping pencils; we all have fiddlers in our class, but what can we do to prevent this behaviour?

○ Often these are anxious children, so try not to be cross with them.

○ It does not necessarily mean they are not listening; draw fiddlers into activities to keep them on task.

○ Give fiddlers a job during teaching time when you need everybody's attention, e.g. holding up a poster, turning the pages of the book, etc.

○ Give fiddlers something to hold that they *can* fiddle with, e.g. Blu-Tack, a marble, a shell; something that will not be a huge distraction to you.

○ Use non-verbal signs and gestures as pointers for the fiddler.

○ Keep activities alive and interesting with plenty of whole-class interaction.

○ Keep rewarding fiddlers when they are still.

○ Try to catch fiddlers being still and make a point of telling them how pleased you are *before* they fiddle; they will remain still for longer.

○ Give fiddlers a buddy to hold hands with during carpet time.

○ Give fiddlers a target to aim for with small rewards along the way.

LIST 101 Sixty-second summary of behaviour management

Without a doubt, behaviour management is fascinating, challenging, frustrating and rewarding. It is a *vast* area of study, as is shown in the range of lists provided. *Our* final challenge is to summarize the main points from all these lists in the next sixty seconds ... *Go*!

○ The only person who can really change the behaviour in the classroom is you! With the help of the children, that is!

○ Every day, every teacher working in the early years experiences some kind of behaviour problem – you are not alone!

○ Children will behave how they have been taught to behave. Where poor behaviour is tolerated or ignored then children will continue to behave in that way. So ... *do something about it*!

○ Only take from the lists strategies you think will work for *your* children in *your* class in *your* school.

○ If a strategy does not work, do not despair! Think about *why* it did not work, considering ways to adapt and modify it so that it *does* work.

○ Always remember it is the *behaviour* of the child you are commenting on and not the *actual* child.

○ Every day should start afresh, even if they are driving you mad at 8.55 am!

○ Above everything else, remember to enjoy your job – it is a *privilege* to be able to teach children.